The Concise Illustrated Book of
Tanks

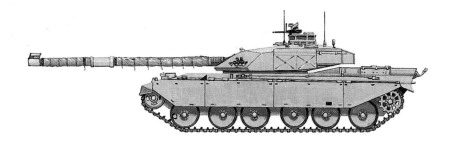

Mark Lloyd

GALLERY BOOKS
An imprint of W. H. Smith Publishers Inc.
112 Madison Avenue
New York, New York 10016

First published in
the United States of America
by GALLERY BOOKS
An imprint of
W.H. Smith Publishers Inc.
112 Madison Avenue
New York, New York 10016

ISBN 0-8317-1691-6

Printed in Portugal

Right:
*An impressive aspect on Britain's Challenger
Mk 2.*

Acknowledgments
All photographs supplied by BTPH with
the exception of the following:
Guy Taylor: page 25
TRH Pictures: page 41
The publishers would also like to thank the
following companies and organizations for
supplying photographs:
Arméstabens bilddetalj, Department of
Defense, General Dynamics Land Systems
Division, Henschel Wehrtechnik, Krauss
Maffei Wehrtechnik, Vickers Defence
Systems.

CONTENTS

INTRODUCTION

Light and main battle tanks (MBTs) have been transformed beyond all recognition since the outbreak of World War II. They have advanced from slow, lightly armed and armoured gun platforms to highly sophisticated weapon systems capable of engaging targets at ranges in excess of 10km (6.2 miles).

Modern tanks are in essence a finely balanced compromise. Ideally they must be fast and manoeuvrable, be heavily armoured and possess sufficient firepower to destroy an enemy MBT on the move. In reality it has rarely proved possible to combine all three facets. Tanks are usually either fast or heavily armoured, rarely both. Traditionally French tanks have been fast and manoeuvrable but at the expense of armoured protection which has been ruthlessly discounted to save weight. Conversely British tanks, notably Centurion and Chieftain, have offered their crews superb protection but the additional armour has made them so heavy that they have proved slow and ponderous on the battlefield. Recent attempts to overcome this problem by fitting far more powerful engines have met with limited success. The 1,500hp gas turbine Lycoming Textron AGT-1500 powerplant fitted to the United States' M1 Abrams has given the 54,432kg (119,750 lb) monster an enviable top speed of 72.5km/h (45 mph) but has proved unacceptably hot and noisy, rendering the tank an easy target for enemy heat-seeking ordnance. Attempts to lighten the weight of armour without compromising its effectiveness have proved more successful. Britain and the United States have fitted their Challenger and Abrams tanks with still secret slab-sided Chobham armour, while the Soviets have now retro-fitted their front-line fighting vehicles with simple but highly effective reactive explosive armour.

The evolution of the tank gun has been steadier but no less dramatic. For two decades the British L7 105mm gun was deemed the finest in the world. It was fitted to the late mark Centurions, to the United States M60, the West German Leopard 1, the Swiss Pz 61 and Pz 68 and was retro-fitted to a host of older tanks. The 115mm (4.55 in) gun fitted to the Soviet T-62, then the Warsaw Pact's principal MBT, was considered to be vastly inferior. However, as armoured protection and anti-tank artillery improved, the need for a more powerful, longer-range gun became apparent. Both West Germany and Britain experimented with new 120mm (4.75 in) calibre proto-types with varying degrees of success. Britain introduced the rifled L11A5 and West Germany the more revolutionary smooth-bore Rheinmetall. Due in part to its superior design, and in part to the excellent associated fire-control system fitted to the Leopard 2 in which it was trialled, the West German gun proved far more popular and is now in service with the Dutch, Swiss and United States' armies. During the last decade the Soviet Union has attempted to overcome the inherent inaccuracy of its tank main armament at long range by introducing barrels capable of accepting both 125mm (4.92 in) rounds and the AT-8 missile, but with very limited success.

Artillery may have been the god of 19th-century war but that position is now held by the tank. No one knows what the future will bring to the battlefield. What is certain is that for the conceivable future there will always be a place for the tank.

AMX-30

Developed originally as a joint Franco-Italian-German enterprise, the entire project was adopted by the French when her partners pulled out. The AMX-30 entered production in 1966 and is now in service with nine countries. It has excellent mobility but limited protection and is therefore of limited use against the latest generation of MBTs. The AMX-30 is fitted with infra-red driving and fighting equipment while the later AMX-30B2 variant is also fitted with laser rangefinder and automatic COTAC integrated fire control system. Unusually the 12.7mm (0.5 in) or 20mm (0.8 in) co-axial machine gun can be elevated independently of the main armament for use against low-flying helicopters.

Type: main battle tank
Nationality: French
Crew: four
Weight: empty 34,000kg (74,960 lb); loaded 36,000kg (79,365 lb)
Dimensions: length (gun forward) 9.48m (31 ft 1 in), (hull) 6.6m (21 ft 8 in); width 3.1m (10 ft 2 in); height 2.86m (9 ft 4 in)
Ground Pressure: 0.77kg/sq cm (10.95 psi)
Performance: road speed 65km/h (40.4 mph); range 650km (404 miles); vertical obstacle 0.93m (3 ft 2 in); trench 2.9m (9 ft 6 in); gradient 60%; wading 2m (6 ft 7 in); with snorkel 4m (13 ft 2 in)
Engine: Hispano-Suiza HS-110 12-cylinder water-cooled, multi-fuel engine developing 700hp at 2,400rpm

Armament: 105mm (4.16 in) CN-105-F1 gun, either 12.7mm (0.5 in) co-axial machine gun or 20mm (0.8 in) cannon, 7.62mm (0.3 in) machine gun, two smoke dischargers
Armour: approximately 50mm (2 in)

Equipped with, perhaps, the most effective 105mm primary armament of any current main battle tank, the AMX-30 has been exported in some numbers.

AMX-32

The AMX-32 was designed specifically as an export variant of the AMX-30B2, itself a development of the AMX-30. The welded turret offers increased protection and more room for the crew with enhanced visibility for the commander provided by a TOP 7VS cupola capable of 360-degree counter-rotation. The 105mm (4.16 in) CN-105-F1 gun is fitted as standard, although provision has been made to replace this with the much advanced French 120mm smooth-bore gun capable of accepting the new APFSDS projectile, together with conventional Rheinmetall 120mm ammunition. The 20mm (0.8 in) cannon can be linked to the main armament or fired independently, while the 7.62mm (0.3 in) machine gun mounted on the commander's cupola can be fired from within the tank.

Type: main battle tank
Nationality: French
Crew: four
Weight: loaded 38,000kg (83,790 lb)
Dimensions: length (gun forward) 9.48m (31 ft 1 in), (hull) 6.59m (21 ft 7 in); width 3.24m (10 ft 7 in); height 2.96m (9 ft 8 in)
Ground Pressure: 0.85kg/sq cm (12.15 psi)
Performance: road speed 65km/h (40.4 mph); range 530km (329 miles); vertical obstacle 0.93m (3 ft); trench 2.9m (9 ft 6 in); gradient 60%
Engine: Hispano-Suiza HS-110-2 12-cylinder multi-fuel developing 800hp at 2,000rpm

Armament: 105mm (4.16 in) gun (optional fitting for 120mm gun), 20mm (0.8 in) co-axial cannon, 7.62mm (0.3 in) A/A machine gun, six smoke dischargers.

Aimed specifically at the export market, the AMX-32 represents a relatively modest advance in terms of overall capability compared with the AMX-30 from which it was developed.

CENTURION MK 10

First developed by AEC Ltd in 1944, the Centurion just failed to see service in World War II. It first saw action in Korea, since which time it has served in battle in India, south Arabia, Vietnam, the Middle East and Suez. Centurion owes much of its success to its capacity to be upgunned and uparmoured to meet the latest requirements, although its slow speed and poor operational range have always proved impediments. In its final form, the Mk 13, it was armed with the highly successful L7A2 105mm (4.16 in) tank gun subsequently fitted to the West German Leopard 1, the early United States Abrams, to all but the latest M 60 variants, and to the Swiss Pz 61 and Pz 68. The gun, with its effective static range of 1,800m (5,906 ft) when firing APDS rounds and 3,500m (11,483 ft) when firing HESH, is ranged using a 12.7mm (0.5 in) ranging gun.

Type: main battle tank
Nationality: United Kingdom
Crew: four
Weight: 51,820kg (114,004 lb)
Dimensions: length (gun forward) 9.85m (32 ft 3 in), (hull) 7.82m (25 ft 7 in); width 3.39m (11 ft 1 in); height 3.009m (9 ft 10 in)
Ground Pressure: 0.95kg/sq cm (13.59 psi)
Performance: speed 34.6km/h (21.5 mph); range 190km (118 miles); vertical obstacle 0.91m (3 ft); trench 3.352m (11 ft); gradient 60%; wading 1.45m (4 ft 6 in)
Engine: Rolls-Royce Meteor Mk IV B 12-cylinder liquid-cooled petrol engine, developing 650hp at 2,550rpm

Armament: 105mm (4.16 in) L7 tank gun, 7.62mm (0.3 in) co-axial machine gun, 12.7mm (0.5 in) machine gun, 7.62mm (0.3 in) A/A machine gun
Armour: 17mm (0.67 in) minimum, 152mm (6.08 in) maximum

Top right:
Still operated in its AVRE form by the British Army, the Centurion was operated by 10 other countries, including Sweden, to whom this 105mm up-gunned example belongs.

CHALLENGER

Challenger's main armament consists of the proven 120mm (4.75 in) L11 semi-automatic gun which, although inferior to the West German Rheinmetall 120mm (4.75 in) smooth-bore, is still highly potent. Bagged or combustible cased ammunition, loaded through a vertically sliding breech and initiated by an electrically primed vent tube, may be fired. Storage allows for up to 64 projectiles and 42 charge containers to be carried. The main gun is targeted with the aid of Challenger's computerized fire-control system which assimilates information on range, target movement, the present course and position, weather and barrel fatigue before calculating main armament lay and bringing the gun into position. The new Rolls-Royce engine, capable of developing 1,200hp, is a vast improvement on the old Leyland L60 and gives Challenger a degree of manoeuvrability previously unknown in British tanks. Protection is enhanced by use of the still secret British-designed Chobham armour while a pressurized filtration system counters the NBC threat. Plans are presently in the pipeline to introduce a new Challenger 2 variant.

Type: main battle tank
Nationality: United Kingdom
Crew: four
Weight: 62,000kg (136,684 lb)
Dimensions: length (gun forward) 11.55m (37 ft 10 in), (hull) 8.39m (27 ft 6 in), (gun rear) 9.86m (32 ft 4 in); width 3.52m (11 ft 6 in); height 2.89m (9 ft 6 in)
Ground Pressure: 0.9kg/sq cm (12.87 psi)

Performance: speed 60km/h (37.2 mph)
Engine: Rolls-Royce CV12 TCA 12-cylinder 60V direct injection, 4-stroke diesel, compression-ignition developing 1,200hp at 2,300 rpm.
Armament: 120mm (4.75 in) L11A5 tank gun, 7.62mm (0.3 in) co-axial machine gun, 7.62mm (0.3 in) L37A2 machine gun, two five-barrel smoke dischargers

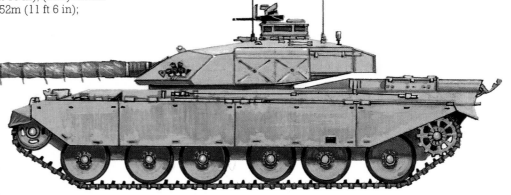

Top right:
Challenger, the British Army's current primary fighting vehicle asset, seen traversing undulating terrain.

CHIEFTAIN

Chieftain entered front-line service with the British Army in 1967 and is still regarded as one of the most powerful fighting tanks in the world. The L60 multi-fuel engine, however, is outdated, under-powered and notoriously unreliable. The Royal Ordnance-manufactured 120mm (4.75 in) L11A5 main armament is operated by a small joystick, controllable either by the gunner or commander, and can be brought to bear whether or not the tank is moving. With a maximum rate of fire of eight to ten rounds for the first minute and six rounds per minute thereafter, and with a maximum stated range of 3,000m (9,842 ft) when firing APDS, and 8,000m (26,247 ft) when firing HESH, the gun is extremely potent. However, in the eyes of many, it is far inferior to the newer West German Rheinmetall 120mm (4.75 in) smooth-bore now arming the Leopard 2 and M1A1 Abrams.

Type: main battle tank
Nationality: United Kingdom
Crew: four
Weight: empty 53,500kg (117,945 lb); loaded 55,000kg (121,252 lb)
Dimensions: length (gun forward) 10.78m (35 ft 4 in), (hull) 7.52m (24 ft 7 in); width 3.66m (12 ft); height 2.9m (9 ft 5 in)
Ground Pressure: 0.90kg/sq cm (12.87 psi)
Performance: speed 48km/h (29.81 mph); range (road) 500km (310 miles), (cross-country) 250km (155 miles); vertical obstacle 0.91m (3 ft); trench 3.15m (10 ft 4 in); gradient 60%; wading 1.07m (3 ft 6 in) without preparation, 4.57m (15 ft) with snorkel

Engine: Leyland L60 No.4 Mark 7A, 2-stroke, compression ignition, 12-cylinder vertically opposed multi-fuel engine developing 750hp at 2,100rpm
Armament: 120mm (4.75 in) L11 A2 rifled tank gun, 7.62mm (0.3 in) co-axial machine gun, 12.7mm (0.5 in) ranging machine gun, 7.62mm (0.3 in) A/A machine gun
Armour: 150mm (5.9 in) maximum

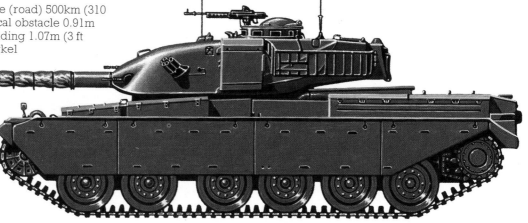

Still in widespread use with the British Army, the Chieftain has, in recent years, been subject to a series of upgradings to both its automotives and sensors.

LEOPARD 1

Arguably the most successful mass production tank since World War II, 4,561 models of the Leopard were built and it is presently in service with ten countries throughout the world. Heavily armoured yet fast, versatile and with an excellent cross-country reputation, the Leopard 1 is highly suited to the central European plains. Armed with the British manufactured 105mm (4.16 in) tank gun, a 7.62mm (0.3 in) MG3 co-axial and 7.62mm (0.3 in) A/A machine gun, and equipped with a stabilization system, night-vision equipment, a thermal sleeve and passive infra-red vision equipment, Leopard 1 is a highly potent fighting machine. Several variants including an armoured recovery vehicle, armoured bridgelayer (the Biber) and anti-aircraft tank (the Gepard) are in existence.

Type: main battle tank
Nationality: West German
Crew: four
Weight: empty 40,400kg (89,066 lb); loaded 42,200kg (93,475 lb)
Dimensions: length (gun forward) 9.54m (31 ft 4 in), (hull) 7.09m (23 ft 3 in); width 3.25m (10 ft 8 in); height 2.64m (8 ft 8 in)
Ground Pressure: 0.9kg/sq cm (12.8 psi)
Performance: road speed 65km/h (40 mph); range 600km (373 miles); vertical obstacle 1.15m (3 ft 9 in); trench 3m (9 ft 10 in); gradient 60%; wading 1.2m (4 ft) without preparation, 2.25m (7 ft 5 in) with preparation, 4m (13 ft 2 in) with snorkel

Engine: 830-hp Daimler-Benz MTU MB 838 Ca M500 supercharged multi-fuel in-line engine
Armament: 105mm (4.16 in) L7A3 gun, 7.62mm (0.3 in) co-axial machine gun, 7.62mm (0.3 in) machine gun, four smoke dischargers either side of turret
Armour: 10mm (0.4 in) minimum, 70mm (2.75 in) maximum

Top right:
Shown here is a Leopard IA-4, the latest variant, incorporating new fire control and thermal imaging systems.

LEOPARD 2

One of the most successful tanks in the world, Leopard 2 enjoys a unique combination of excellent mobility, massive firepower and strong armoured protection. Currently in service with West Germany, Holland and Switzerland, it began its design life as a multinational concept but was ultimately developed by Krauss-Maffei of Munich. The Rheinmetall 120mm smooth-bore gun, now also fitted to the M1A1 Abrams, will fire an armour piercing discarding sabot round capable of penetrating non-reactive MBT armour at ranges in excess of 2,200m (7,215 ft). An advanced fire-control system coupled with a combined laser and stereoscopic rangefinder, together with full stabilization, give an excellent first-round hit probability on the move. A full NBC system, heaters and a passive infra-red night system are standard.

Type: main battle tank
Nationality: West German
Crew: four
Weight: (loaded) 56,600kg (124,780 lb)
Dimensions: length (gun forward) 9.74m (31 ft 11 in); (hull) 7.73m (25 ft 4 in); width (with skirts) 3.54m (11 ft 7 in); height (turret top) 2.49m (8 ft)
Ground Pressure: 0.86kg/sq cm (12.23 psi)
Performance: road speed 68km/h (42 mph); range 500km (310 miles); vertical obstacle 1.15m (3 ft 9 in); trench 3.1m (10 ft 2 in); gradient 60%; wading 1.1m (3 ft 7 in) without preparation, 2.25m (7 ft 4 in) with preparation, 4m (13 ft 2 in) with snorkel

Engine: MTU MB 873 Ka 501 12-cylinder water-cooled multi-fuel engine developing 1,500hp at 2,600rpm
Armament: 120mm (4.75 in) smooth-bore Rheinmetall gun, 7.62mm (0.3 in) MG3 co-axial machine gun, 7.62mm (0.3 in) A/A machine gun, eight smoke dischargers on each side of turret
Armour: classified but of Chobham design

Top right:
The highly effective Leopard II, seen here demonstrating its ability to traverse ground almost as fast backwards as forward.

M1 ABRAMS

M1 Abrams was designed in the 1970s specifically to counter the latest generation of Soviet tanks. Initial models were armed with the M68 105mm (4.16 in) British designed tank gun but these are now being replaced with the far superior 120mm Rheinmetall smooth-bore. Protection is provided by layers of still secret British Chobham armour, which it is claimed makes Abrams immune to the majority of anti-tank guns and missiles in the Soviet armoury. Although the Lycoming Textron engine and Allison X1100-3B transmission are extremely reliable and require little field servicing, they are extremely noisy and hot, giving the tank a dangerous 'signature' to enemy infra-red and radar. The gun is fully stabilized with an excellent laser rangefinder. All models are NBC proofed and provided with a full range of night-vision equipment for the commander, gunner and driver.

Type: main battle tank
Nationality: United States
Crew: four
Weight: 54,432kg (119,750 lb)
Dimensions: length (gun forward) 9.76m (32 ft), (hull) 7.92m (26 ft); width 3.66m (12 ft); height 2.89m (9 ft 6 in) to top of turret
Ground Pressure: 0.96kg/sq cm (13.7 psi)
Performance: road speed 72.5km/h (45 mph); cross country 48.5km/h (30 mph); range 450km (280 miles); vertical obstacle 1.24m (4 ft 1 in); trench 2.74m (9 ft); gradient 60%

Engine: Lycoming Textron AGT-1500 1500hp gas turbine developing 1,500hp at 3,000rpm
Armament: 105mm (4.16 in) or Rheinmetall 120mm (4.75 in) tank gun, two × 7.62mm (0.3 in) machine guns (one co-axial, commander's cupola and loader's hatch), 12.7mm (0.5 in) A/A machine gun

Top right:
The M1A2, seen here, has been up-gunned with the smooth-bore 120mm, in place of the earlier M1A1's 105mm gun.

M47

In many respects a modernized variant of the World War II M26 Pershing heavy tank, the M47 was developed for, but did not see service in, the Korean War. Too lightly armed and armoured for central European service, the M47 was replaced within a year in American service by the M48 but not until 8,676 models had been built, mainly for export under the United States Mutual Aid Program. The main armament is the M36 90mm (3.56 in) tank gun fitted with either a T-shaped or cylindrical blast deflector. Although smoke and anti-personnel rounds can be fired to ranges in excess of 20,000m (65,617 ft), maximum elevation is required making re-loading slow and arduous. More fundamentally, anti-tank HEAT-T and AP-T rounds have effective ranges of less than 2,000m (6,561 ft), leaving the tank highly vulnerable to modern MBTs and anti-tank guns.

Type: medium tank
Nationality: United States
Crew: five
Weight: empty 42,130kg (92,879 lb); loaded 46,170kg (101,775 lb)
Dimensions: length (gun forward) 8.51m (28 ft 1 in), (hull) 6.31m (20 ft 8 in); width 3.51m (10 ft 6 in); height 3.35m (11 ft) including anti-aircraft machine gun
Ground Pressure: 0.94kg/sq cm (13.3 psi)
Performance: speed 58km/h (36 mph); range 130km (80 miles); vertical obstacle 0.91m (3 ft); trench 2.59m (8 ft); gradient 60%; wading 1.22m (4 ft)

This Italian M47 was one of many supplied as part of US military aid to its allies.

Engine: Continental AV-1790-5B 12-cylinder air-cooled petrol engine developing 810hp at 2,800rpm
Armament: 90mm (3.56 in) M36 tank gun, 7.62mm (0.3 in) M1919A4E1 machine guns (co-axial and bow), 12.7mm (0.5 in) M2 machine gun on commander's cupola
Armour: 12.7mm (0.5 in) minimum, 115mm (4.6 in) maximum

M48

Essentially an improved version of the M47, the first M48 medium tank entered service in 1953. Armed with the same 90mm (3.56 in) cannon, but with a far stronger hull and turret, it was a vast improvement. Simple to manufacture and reliable to operate, the basic M48 Patton has been heavily updated by a number of NATO and Middle Eastern countries with whom it remains in front-line service. The M48A3 was retro-fitted with a diesel engine to increase its operational range and with an enhanced fire-control system to improve safety. Subsequently the M48A5, presently in service with such countries as Greece, Turkey and Portugal, was fitted with the more powerful British L7 105mm (4.16 in) tank gun, new tracks and a modernized 7.62mm (0.3 in) M60D co-axial machine gun.

Type: medium tank
Nationality: United States
Crew: four
Weight: empty 42,240m (93,122 lb); loaded 47,174kg (104,000 lb)
Dimensions: length (gun forward) 8.44m (27 ft 8 in), (hull) 6.88m (22 ft 7 in); width 3.63m (11 ft 11 in); height 3.12m (10 ft 3 in)
Ground Pressure: 0.83kg/sq cm (11.8 psi)
Performance: speed 48km/h (30 mph); range 463km (288 miles); vertical obstacle 0.95m (3 ft); trench 2.59m (8 ft 6 in); gradient 60%; wading 1.22m (4 ft) without preparation, 2.44m (8 ft) with snorkel
Engine: Continental AVDS-1790-2A 12-cylinder air-cooled diesel developing 750hp at 2,400rpm

Armament: 90mm (3.56 in) M41 tank gun, 7.62mm (0.3 in) M73 co-axial machine gun, 12.7mm (0.5 in) machine gun mounted on commander's cupola
Armour: 12.7mm (0.5 in) minimum, 120mm (4.8 in) maximum

Top right:
Two German Army M48A3 tank commanders pause to exchange notes.

16

M60

The M60 was the last development of the M47/M48 family and perhaps the most successful tank ever to be produced in the United States. It differed from its immediate predecessors in having a 105mm (4.16 in) gun (derived from the British L7 but built domestically under licence), a diesel engine, and greatly enhanced turret armour. Although the original M60 entered service in 1959 the initial basic combat model was the M60A1 with a sloping turret designed to offer greater protection against anti-tank missiles. During the early 1980s it was decided to extend the life of the M60 by introducing the M60A3 which incorporated a gun stabilization system, a laser rangefinder in place of the coincidence optical system, a solid-state ballistic computer, improved tracks, and a more reliable powerplant and electrics. The M60 is now being phased out of United States service in favour of the M1A1 Abrams.

Type: main battle tank
Nationality: United States
Crew: four
Weight: empty 42,184kg (92,998 lb); loaded 48,987kg (108,000 lb)
Dimensions: (gun forward) 9.31m (30 ft 6 in), (hull) 6.94m (22 ft 10 in); width 3.36m (11 ft 11 in); height 3.26m (10 ft 8 in)
Ground Pressure: 0.79kg/sq cm (11.24 psi)
Performance: speed 48km/h (30 mph); range 500km (310 miles); vertical obstacle 0.91m (3 ft); trench 2.59m (8 ft 6 in); gradient 60%; wading 1.22m (4 ft) unprepared, 2.44m (8 ft) with equipment, 4.11m (13 ft 6 in) with snorkel

Engine: Continental AVDS-1790-2A 12-cylinder diesel developing 750hp at 2,400rpm
Armament: 105mm (4.16 in) tank gun, 7.62mm (0.3 in) co-axial machine gun, 12.7mm (0.5 in) A/A machine gun
Armour: 12.7mm (0.5 in) minimum, 120mm (4.8 in) maximum

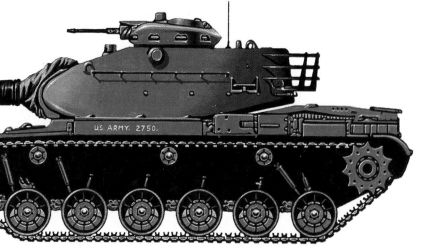

Top right:
The upgraded TTS version of the M60A3.

MERKAVA

Merkava (Chariot) entered service with the Israeli Defence Forces in 1978. Designed specifically to counter the threat of Arab armour and anti-tank weaponry, it contains a number of unique features. The American Teledyne engine is forward mounted to offer the crew a degree of protection during frontal assaults. The small, well-sloped turret is situated towards the rear, while the rear compartment itself may be used as an additional crew compartment to ferry infantrymen into battle or casevac the wounded to the rear. Main armament consists of the 105mm (4.16 in) 7 series rifled tank gun with fume extractor and thermal sleeve. Variants include the Mk 2 with hydropneumatic suspension and the Mk 3 with a more powerful main armament. Due to the great weight of its armour the Merkava is slow and liable to bog down when operating in soft sand.

Type: main battle tank
Nationality: Israeli
Crew: four
Weight: 58,000kg (127,890 lb)
Dimensions: length (with gun) 8.63m (28 ft 4 in), (hull) 7.45m (24 ft 5 in); width 3.7m (12 ft 7 in); height 2.64m (8 ft 9 in) to top of commander's cupola
Ground Pressure: 0.9kg.sq cm (12.8 psi)
Performance: road speed 58km/h (36 mph); range 400km (248 miles); vertical obstacle 0.92m (3 ft); trench 3.2m (10 ft 6 in); gradient 60%; wading 1.38m (4 ft 6 in) without preparation, 2m (6 ft 7 in) with preparation

Engine: Teledyne Continental AVDS-1790–5A V-12 diesel developing 900hp at 2,400rpm
Armament: 105mm (4.16 in) gun (120mm in Mk 3s), 7.62mm (0.3 in) co-axial machine gun, 2 × 7.62mm (0.3 in) A/A fire control system, 60mm (2.36 in) roof-mounted mortar, smoke dischargers

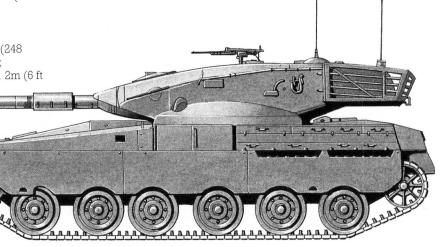

Israel's Merkava, one of the world's heaviest armed and armoured main battle tanks.

OF-40

The OF-40 is the latest in a long series of excellent Italian weapon systems. Developed by OTO-Melara in conjunction with Fiat, the first models entered service in 1981, only a year after the first prototype. The 105mm (4.16 in) gun will accept all conventional NATO APDS, HEAT and HESH rounds. A laser rangefinder and roof-mounted SFIM 580-B sight give an excellent first-round hit capability. Automatic fire extinguishing and NBC over-pressure systems enable the crew to operate the versatile OF-40 in relative comfort and safety. An anti-aircraft turret and alternative weapon systems have been fitted to a number of variants.

Type: main battle tank
Nationality: Italian
Crew: four
Weight: empty 40,000kg (88,185 lb); loaded 43,000kg (94,798 lb)
Dimensions: length (gun forward) 9.22m (30 ft 3 in), (hull) 6.89m (22 ft 7 in); width 3.51m (11 ft 6 in) with skirts; height 2.68m (8 ft 11 in) to top of commander's cupola
Ground Pressure: 0.86kg/sq cm (12.3 psi)
Performance: speed 60km/h (37.25 mph); range 600km (372 miles); vertical obstacle 1.1m (3 ft 7 in); gradient 60%; wading 1.2m (3 ft 11 in) without preparation, 2.25m (7 ft 5 in) with preparation, 4m (13 ft 2 in) with snorkel
Engine: 90 V-10 supercharged multi-fuel engine developing 830hp at 2,200rpm

Armament: 105mm (4.16 in) gun, 7.62mm (0.3 in) co-axial machine gun, 7.62mm (0.3 in) A/A machine gun, four smoke dischargers either side of turret

Top right:
An impressive frontal aspect of Italy's OF-40, showing something of its Leopard I design influence.

PANZER 68

Until recently Switzerland felt it incumbent upon her neutrality where possible not to purchase armaments from either of the major blocs. The Pz 61 entered service in 1964 and was followed seven years later by the updated Pz 68. Main armament consists of a British designed modified 105mm (4.16 in) L7 tank gun fitted with a thermal sleeve in later variants and made under licence in Switzerland. A laser rangefinder and stabilizer enable the Pz 68 to engage targets while on the move. Rubber pads fitted to the tracks and infra-red driving lights offer an all-weather capability and an NBC system is fitted as standard. Switzerland has now ceased tank production and has recently taken delivery of a consignment of West German Leopard 2 MBTs.

Although succeeded in front-line Swiss service by the Leopard II, the indigenously-designed and developed Pz68 continues in supporting roles.

Type: main battle tank
Nationality: Swiss
Crew: four
Weight: loaded 39,700kg (87,522 lb); empty 38,700kg (85,317 lb)
Dimensions: length (gun forward) 9.49m (31 ft 2 in), (hull) 6.9m (22 ft 8 in); width 3.14m (10 ft 3 in); height 2.74m (9 ft) to top of cupola
Ground Pressure: 0.86kg/sq cm (12.1 psi)
Performance: speed 55km/h (34 mph); range 350km (217 miles); vertical obstacle 75cm (2 ft 6 in); trench 2.6m (8 ft 6 in); gradient 70%; wading 1.12m (3 ft 8 in) without preparation
Engine: MTU MB 837 8-cylinder developing 704hp at 2,200rpm
Armament: 105mm (4.16 in) tank gun, 7.5mm (0.3 in) co-axial machine gun, 7.5mm (0.3 in) A/A machine gun, two triple smoke dischargers
Armour: 20mm (0.78 in) minimum to 60mm (2.36 in) maximum

STRIDSVAGN 103

One of the most unusual and controversial tanks ever designed, the Bofors S Tank, the only modern MBT to be built without a turret, has not been a total success. The 105mm (4.16 in) L7 gun, with its automatic loader, is located in the hull. The barrel can be raised and depressed between +12 and −10 degrees with the aid of hydro-pneumatic suspension. Traverse of the main armament is effected by slewing the tank on its tracks and using the auxiliary engine when the tank has been brought to a halt in approximately the right direction. Optical and laser rangefinders, night vision equipment and a flotation screen (which can be erected in 15 minutes) are fitted but there is no NBC protection. Reloading the 50-round magazines takes approximately ten minutes. In the hands of an experienced crew, the automatic loader will allow a rate of fire of 12 rounds per minute.

Type: main battle tank
Nationality: Swedish
Crew: three
Weight: 39,000kg (85,980 lb)
Dimensions: length (including armament) 9.8m (32 ft 1 in), (hull) 7m (23 ft); width 3.6m (12 ft); height 2.5m (8 ft 3 in)
Ground Pressure: 0.9kg/sq cm (12.8 psi)
Performance: road speed 50km/h (31 mph); water speed 6km/h (4 mph); range 390km (242 miles); vertical obstacle 0.9m (2 ft 11 in); trench 2.3m (7 ft 7 in); gradient 60%; wading 1.5m (4 ft 11 in) without preparation

The S Tank offers the smallest target area to any opponent, both in terms of frontal and side-on aspects.

Armament: 105mm (4.16 in) L7A1 L/62 rifled tank gun, two 7.62mm (0.3 in) FN machine guns on a pack on the left track guard, 7.62mm (0.3 in) A/A machine gun

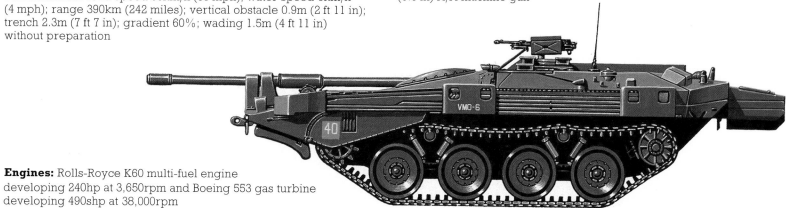

Engines: Rolls-Royce K60 multi-fuel engine developing 240hp at 3,650rpm and Boeing 553 gas turbine developing 490shp at 38,000rpm

T-34/85

Derived in 1943 from the earlier T-34/76B, the T-34/85 was without doubt the premier mass-production tank of World War II. Although phased out of the Soviet Army in the mid-1950s, production of an updated version of the T34/85, with a new engine and wheels, continued on a limited scale until 1964, by which time an estimated 50,000 models had been built. The tank remains in service with a number of smaller countries throughout North and Central Africa, the Far and Middle East and South-east Asia. Designed for wartime production on a vast scale, the constituent parts have been kept as cheap and simple as possible. No consideration has been given to comfort, the five-man crew being expected to operate in and forward of the small, cramped centrally positioned turret. The bow-mounted 7.62mm (0.3 in) machine gun, operated by the fifth member of the crew seated to the right of the driver, gave the tank added potency against the lightly equipped remnants of the German infantry during the final stages of the war. A number of variants, including the Czech MT-34 armoured bridgelayer, T-34-T armoured recovery vehicle and SKP-5 armoured crane, were developed and remain in limited numbers in the reserve.

Soviet infantry advances in the tracks of a T-34.

Type: main battle tank
Nationality: Soviet Union
Crew: five
Weight: 32,000kg (70,547 lb)
Dimensions: length (gun forward) 8.08m (25 ft 8 in), (hull) 6.0m (19 ft 9 in); width 3m (9 ft 10 in); height 2.74m (9 ft)
Ground Pressure: 0.8kg/sq cm (11.2 psi)
Performance: speed 50km/h (31 mph); range 300km (186 miles); vertical obstacle 79cm (2 ft 9 in); trench 2.49m (8 ft 2 in); gradient 60%; wading 1.32m (4 ft 4 in) without preparation
Engine: model V-2-34 or V-2-34M, V-12, water-cooled diesel developing 500hp at 1,800rpm.
Armament: 85mm (3.37 in) M-1944 (ZIS-S53) gun, 7.62mm (0.3 in) co-axial machine gun, 7.62mm (0.3 in) DTM machine gun mounted in the bow
Armour: 18mm (0.71 in) minimum; 90mm (3.54 in) maximum

T-55

The T-55 was developed in 1947 but did not enter production until 1950. Since then it has been produced under licence in at least four countries and is still being built in an updated form as the T-59 in Communist China. In all over 50,000 models were constructed. The T-55 saw action in the streets of Warsaw in 1956 and was used extensively by the North Vietnamese Army in its war against Saigon. The D-10T2S tank gun, a development of a World War II naval gun, would be of limited use against modern main battle tanks, a problem made worse by the fact that it can be depressed only to −4° and cannot therefore adopt a conventional hull-down defensive position. India and Israel retain a number of T-55s retro-fitted with either the Soviet 115mm (4.55 in) or British L7 105mm (4.16 in) tank gun, while variants such as the Czech-built MT-55 armoured bridgelayer remain in Soviet service.

A trio of Egyptian T-55s on parade.

Type: main battle tank
Nationality: Soviet Union
Crew: four
Weight: 36,000kg (79,366 lb)
Dimensions: length (gun forward) 9m (29 ft 6 in), (hull) 6.45m (21 ft 2 in); width 3.27m (10 ft 9 in); height 2.4m (7 ft 10 in) without anti-aircraft gun
Ground Pressure: 0.81kg/sq cm (11.52 psi)

Armament: 100mm (3.6 in) tank gun, 7.62mm (0.3 in) co-axial machine gun, 7.62mm (0.3 in) bow-gun, 12.7mm (0.5 in) A/A machine gun
Armour: 20mm (0.79 in) minimum, 170mm (6.69 in) maximum

Performance: speed 48km/h (30 mph); range 400km (249 miles): vertical obstacle 0.8m (2 ft 8 in); trench 2.7m (8 ft 10 in); gradient 60%; wading 1.4m (4 ft 7 in), 5.48m (18 ft) with snorkel
Engine: model V-54 V-12 water-cooled diesel developing 520hp at 2,000rpm.

T-62

The T-62 entered production in late 1961 but was not seen publicly until the Moscow May Day Parade of 1965. Basically a larger variant of the T-55 designed to accommodate the U-5T tank gun, the T-62 has several shortcomings. It saw action in the hands of the Syrians and Egyptians during the Middle East War of October 1973 but proved no match for the Western manufactured Israeli armour. The main armament is slow to load and offers no more than 33 per cent accuracy at maximum range. The automatic ejection system, introduced because the interior is too small to permit the ejection of shell cases internally, often malfunctions, causing spent cases to career into the turret and occasionally cause serious injury to the crew. An improved version was introduced in 1965 incorporating easier access to the transmission and facilitating the fitting of engine seals for deep wading. Snorkelling, however, remains dangerous and highly unpopular with the crews as no means of escape exists from the tank once submerged. Over 20,000 T-62s were produced in the Soviet Union, and another 1,500 in Czechoslovakia, although the tank never served with Soviet forces abroad.

Type: main battle tank
Nationality: Soviet Union
Crew: four
Weight: 37,500kg (82,673 lb)
Dimensions: length (gun forward) 9.77m (32 ft), (hull) 6.63m (21 ft 9 in); width 3.35m (11 ft); height 2.4m (7 ft 10 in) without anti-aircraft machine gun
Ground Pressure: 0.72kg/sq cm (10.24 psi)

An Egyptian T-62; note the twin SAKR launcher.

Armament: 115mm (4.55 in) U-5TS tank gun, 7.62mm (0.3 in) PKT co-axial machine gun, 12.7mm (0.5 in) anti-aircraft machine gun (on T-62A only)
Armour: 20mm (0.78 in) minimum, 170mm (6.69 in) maximum

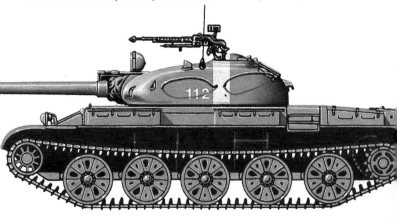

Performance: speed 55km/h (34 mph); range 480km (298 miles); vertical obstacle 80cm (2 ft 10 in); trench 2.8m (9 ft 2 in); gradient 60%; wading 1.6m (4 ft 7 in) without preparation, 3.96m (13 ft) with snorkel
Engine: model V-2-62 12-cylinder water-cooled diesel engine developing 700hp at 2,200rpm

T-64

T-64 entered service with the Soviet Army in the mid 1960s and is now being withdrawn as part of Gorbachev's policy of armament reductions. The new 125mm (4.92 in) D-81T smooth-bore tank gun has not proved overly successful due to its susceptibility to thermal barrel distortion and crosswind interference at ranges in excess of 1,500m (4,921 ft.) More fundamentally, the automatic loader has proved unreliable, having demonstrated an unfortunate tendency to load carelessly positioned hands together with the consumable case ammunition. Soviet attempts to circumvent the inadequacy of the tank gun with the introduction of a tube-fired, anti-tank guided missile have proved no more successful. Code-named 'Kobra' and known to NATO as AT-8, the new missile, designed to be fired from the barrel of the T-64B variant, is believed to lack both accuracy and penetration at long range. The T-64's revolutionary opposed-piston engine and suspension was so expensive to produce and maintain that it proved impractical to export the tank to the non-Soviet Warsaw Pact members.

Soviet T-64Bs and their crews.

Type: main battle tank
Nationality: Soviet Union
Crew: three
Weight: 38,000kg (83,774 lb)
Dimensions: length (gun forward) 9.02m (29 ft 7 in), (hull) 6.4m (21 ft); width 4.64m (15 ft 2 in) with skirts, 3.38m (11 ft 1 in) without skirts; height 2.4m (7 ft 10 in)
Ground Pressure: 1.09kg/sq cm (15.58 psi)
Performance: speed 70km/h (43.5 mph); range 500km (310 miles)

Armour: 20mm (0.78 in) minimum, 250mm (9.84 in) maximum

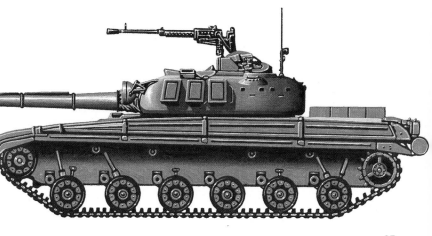

with internal fuel, 600km (373 miles) with supplementary tanks; vertical obstacle 80cm (2 ft 7 in); trench 2.7m (8 ft 10 in); gradient 60%; wading 1.4m (4 ft 7 in)
Engine: 5-cylinder opposed piston diesel, liquid-cooled, developing 750hp at 3,000rpm.
Armament: D-81T 125mm (4.92 in) tank gun, 7.62mm (0.3 in) PKT co-axial machine gun, 12.7mm (0.5 in) NSVT anti-aircraft machine gun

T-72

T-72 entered production in 1972 and is still being produced at the rate of approximately 2,000 tanks per annum in the Soviet Union, Poland and Czechoslovakia. With the T-72 similar in many respects to the T-64 the modifications that do exist are more regressive than evolutionary. The opposed-piston engine has been replaced with the tried and tested and far cheaper V-46 turbo-charged version of the V-2 diesel engine in service since 1938. The complicated suspension of the T-64 has been replaced with a conventional torsion bar system first employed on the T-55. The T-72M variant, first introduced in 1975, was retro-fitted with fabric armour skirts on the hull, thickened frontal turret armour and a laser rangefinder in place of the older optical rangefinder. More recent variants have appeared with smoke dischargers, anti-radiation lining and, most recently, explosive reactive armour.

Type: main battle tank
Nationality: Soviet Union
Crew: three
Weight: 41,000kg (90,388 lb)
Dimensions: length (gun forward) 9.02m (29 ft 7 in), (hull) 6.9m (22 ft 7 in); width 4.75m (15 ft 7 in) with skirts, 3.6m (11 ft 9 in) without skirts; height 2.37m (7 ft 9 in)
Ground Pressure: 0.83kg/sq cm (11.87 psi)
Performance: speed 70km/h (43.4 mph); range 500km (310 miles) with internal fuel, 600km (373 miles) with supplementary tanks; vertical obstacle 1.2m (3 ft 11 in); trench 2.8m (9 ft 2 in); gradient 60%; wading 1.4m (4 ft 7 in)

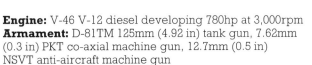

Engine: V-46 V-12 diesel developing 780hp at 3,000rpm
Armament: D-81TM 125mm (4.92 in) tank gun, 7.62mm (0.3 in) PKT co-axial machine gun, 12.7mm (0.5 in) NSVT anti-aircraft machine gun
Armour: 20mm (0.78 in) minimum, 250mm (9.84 in) maximum

T-80

T-80 incorporates many of the design improvements introduced into the later production batches of the T-64 including smoke mortars and enhanced armour. The engine and suspension system are, however, completely new. The 1,000hp turbine engine offers excellent speed and manoeuvrability, while the rubber road wheels, in place of the T-64's unusual Tseits resilient steel wheels, offer a far smoother and quieter ride. Other T-80 improvements include a new laser range-finder and an anti-PGM electronic warfare system. Two versions of the T-80 exist, one with the normal 125mm (4.92 in) 2A46 tank gun and the other capable of firing the AT-8 Kobra anti-tank missile first seen on the T-64B. Without doubt T-80 represents a great advance in Soviet technology, particularly in the fields of mobility and armoured protection. Its firepower is, however, still some considerable way behind that of the latest generation of NATO tanks. Although it enjoys fire-on-the-move capability, it lacks thermal sights, and it would therefore have difficulty in spotting a moving enemy tank while on the move itself during the fog and confusion of modern battle.

Type: main battle tank
Nationality: Soviet Union
Crew: three
Weight: 42,000kg (92,592.5 lb)

Dimensions: length (gun forward) 9.2m (30 ft 2 in), (hull) 7m (22 ft 11 in); width 3.5m (11 ft 5 in); height 2.25m (7 ft 4 in)
Ground Pressure: 0.85kg/sq cm (12.1 psi)
Performance: speed 70km/h (43.5 mph); range 450km (280 miles) with internal fuel, 600km (373 miles) with supplementary tanks; vertical obstacle 80cm (2 ft 7 in); trench 2.7m (8 ft 10 in); gradient 60%; wading 1.4m (4 ft 7 in)
Engine: air-cooled diesel developing 1,000hp

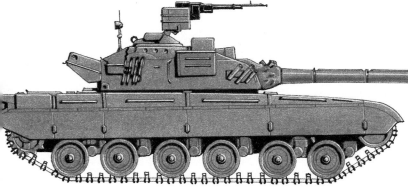

Armament: D-81TM 125mm (4.92 in) tank gun, 7.62mm (0.3 in) PKT co-axial machine gun, 12.7mm (0.5 in) NSVT anti-aircraft machine gun
Armour: 20mm (0.78 in) minimum, 350mm (13.77 in) maximum

Soviet T-80s; note the tile-like reactive armour.

TAM

Although initially built by the West German company of Thyssen Henschel the TAM (Tanque Argentino Mediano) was designed specifically for the Argentine military market and is now being constructed under licence in that country. Based heavily on the chassis of the Marder MICV the heavily sloping hull and turret are of all-steel construction. The 105mm (4.16 in) main armament will accept APFSDS, HEAT, HE-T, HESH and WP-T rounds and is supported by a 7.62mm (0.3 in) co-axial machine gun. Fire control consists of a coincidence rangefinder and commander's panoramic sight with magnification of ×6 to ×20. Fuel is normally stored internally although two long-range tanks may be mounted at the rear of the hull.

Type: medium tank
Nationality: West German/Argentine
Crew: four
Weight: loaded 30,500kg (67,240 lb)
Dimensions: length (gun forward) 8.17m (26 ft 10 in), (hull) 6.57m (21 ft 7 in); width 3.31m (10 ft 10 in); height 2.4m (7 ft 11 in)
Ground Pressure: 0.79kg.sq cm (11.23 psi)
Performance: road speed 75km/h (47 mph); range 600km (373 miles) or 1,000km (621 miles) with auxiliary fuel tanks; vertical obstacle 1m (3 ft 3 in); trench 2.5m (8 ft 3 in); gradient 60%; wading 0.5m (4 ft 11 in) without preparation and 4m (13 ft 2 in) with snorkel

Engine: MTU MB 833 Ka500 supercharged 6-cylinder diesel developing 750hp at 2,200rpm
Armament: 105mm (4.16 in) L7A3 gun, 7.62mm (0.3 in) co-axial machine gun, 7.62mm (0.3 in) A/A machine gun, eight smoke dischargers

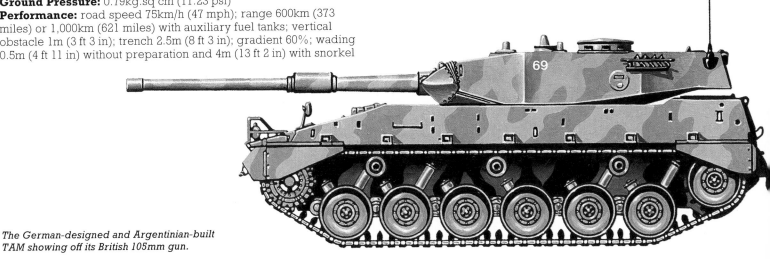

The German-designed and Argentinian-built TAM showing off its British 105mm gun.

TYPE 61

The Type 61, which entered service in 1961, was the first post-war Japanese tank. Based extensively on the United States' M47 medium tank, the Type 61, with its domestically produced 90mm (3.56 in) gun, is lightly armed by modern standards. It was, however, designed exclusively for the home market and had to be small and light enough to be transportable on the Japanese railways with their numerous narrow tunnels. The tank is capable of wading to a depth of 1m (3 ft 3 in) without preparation but unusually has no scope for snorkelling. Late models have been retro-fitted with infra-red driving lights and searchlight to offer a limited night operational facility. Three basic variants exist, the Type 67 Armoured Scissors Bridgelayer, the Type 70 Armoured Recovery Vehicle and an Armoured Engineering Vehicle.

Type: main battle tank
Nationality: Japanese
Crew: four
Weight: 35,000kg (77,162 lb)
Dimensions: length (gun forward) 8.19m (26 ft 11 in), (hull) 6.3m (20 ft 8 in); width 2.95m (9 ft 8 in); height 3.16m (10 ft 4 in) to top of A/A machine gun
Ground Pressure: 0.95kg/sq cm (13.5 psi)
Performance: speed 45km/h (28 mph); range 200km (124 miles); vertical obstacle 0.68m (2 ft 3 in); trench 2.49m (8 ft 2 in); gradient 60%; wading 1m (3 ft 3 in) without preparation
Engine: Mitsubishi Type 12 HM 21 12-cylinder diesel developing 600hp at 2,100rpm
Armament: 90mm (3.56 in) gun, 7.62mm (0.3 in) M1919A4 co-axial machine gun, 12.7mm (0.5 in) M2 A/A gun
Armour: 64mm (2.52 in) maximum

Top right:
A Type 61 on parade at Asaka, Japan, in 1976.

TYPE 74

The Type 74 MBT entered Japanese service in 1973 as a supplement to the undergunned Type 61. The hydro-pneumatic suspension allows the chassis to be raised from a ground clearance of just under 20cm (8 in) to 65cm (2 ft 2 in) giving the vehicle excellent cross-country properties. The front and back may be moved independently, the depression of the front and elevation of the back giving the British designed L7 tank gun, manufactured under licence in Japan, excellent 'hull-down' depression. Fitted with full NBC proofing, with a Nippon Electric laser rangefinder and Mitsubishi Electric ballistic computer, the stabilized main armament is capable of great accuracy when fired on the move.

Type: main battle tank
Nationality: Japanese
Crew: four
Weight: 38,000kg (83,776lb)
Dimensions: length (gun forward) 9.41m (30 ft 10 in), (hull) 6.85m (22 ft 6 in); width 3.18m (10 ft 5 in); height 2.68m (8 ft 10 in) with A/A machine gun
Ground Pressure: 0.85kg/sq cm (12 psi)
Performance: speed 53km/h (33 mph); range 300km (186 miles); vertical obstacle 1m (3 ft 3 in); trench 2.7m (8 ft 10 ft); gradient 60%; wading 1m (3 ft 3 in) without preparation, 3m (9 ft 10 in) with snorkel
Engine: Mitsubishi 10ZF Model 21 WT 10-cylinder air-cooled diesel developing 750hp at 2,200rpm

Armament: 105mm (4.16 in) L7 rifled gun; 7.62mm (0.3 in) co-axial machine gun; 12.7mm (0.5 in) A/A machine gun; six smoke dischargers

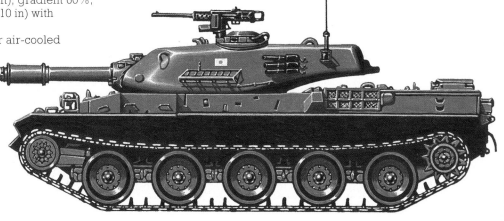

The Japanese Type 74 provided yet another platform for the British 105mm L7 gun.

UPGRADED CENTURION

Early Centurions, including those first supplied to Israel in 1959, had excellent firepower but minimal speed and range. In 1970 the antiquated Rolls-Royce Meteor Mk IVB petrol engines were removed and far more powerful American Teledyne Continental diesel engines retro-fitted. During the refits the rear of the hull was enlarged to offer additional crew space and elevated top decks added to accommodate air vents. New fire-extinguishing and electrical systems were also added. The highly successful British L7 rifled tank gun is retained as main armament.

Type: main battle tank
Nationality: Israeli
Crew: four
Weight: 51,820kg (114,243 lb)
Dimensions: length (gun forward) 9.85m (32 ft 4 in), (hull) 7.82m (25 ft 8 in); width 3.39m (14 ft 1 in); height 3m (9 ft 10 in) to turret roof
Ground Pressure: 0.95kg/sq cm (13.58 psi)
Performance: speed 43km/h (26.7 mph); range 380km (226 miles); vertical obstacle 0.91m (3 ft); trench 3.35m (11 ft); gradient 60%
Engine: Teledyne Continental AVDS-1790-2A diesel developing 900hp at 2,400rpm
Armament: 105mm (4.16 in) L7 rifled tank gun, 12.7mm (0.5 in) RMG, 7.62mm (0.3 in) co-axial machine gun, 7.62mm (0.3 in) A/A machine gun, twin six-barrelled smoke dischargers

Armour: 17mm (0.67 in) minimum to 152mm (6 in) maximum

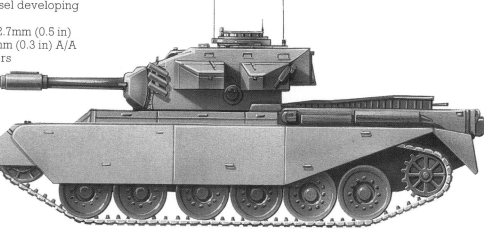

These Israeli Centurions proved formidable opponents in the 1973 war.

VICKERS MAIN BATTLE TANK

Originally designed in the late 1950s as a potential replacement for the Centurion, the Vickers MBT was rejected by Britain in favour of the Chieftain. It was, however, sold to Kuwait and built under licence in India where, to date, over 2,200 models have been built and have entered service under the local name 'Vijayanta'. The original Mk 1 was powered by the tried and tested Leyland L60 6-cylinder water-cooled multi-fuel engine but this was replaced in the updated Mk 3 variant by the more powerful General Motors 12V-71T diesel. The ultra-reliable L7 tank gun has been fitted with the GEC-Marconi gun-control and stabilization system type EC517, affording it extreme accuracy to its maximum range of 5,500m (18,047 ft) when firing HESH or 1,800m (5,906 ft) when firing APDS.

Type: main battle tank
Nationality: United Kingdom
Crew: four
Weight: empty 37,500kg (82,672 lb); loaded 40,000kg (88,183 lb)
Dimensions: length (gun forward) 9.79m (32 ft 1 in), (hull) 7.56m (24 ft 9 in); width 3.17m (10 ft 4 in); height 2.71m (8 ft 10 in)
Ground Pressure: 0.87kg/sq cm (12.44 psi)
Performance: speed 53km/h (33 mph); range 600km (373 miles); vertical obstacle 0.91m (3 ft); trench 2.44m (8 ft); gradient 60%; wading 1.14m (3 ft 9 in)
Engine: General Motors 12V-71T turbo-charged diesel developing 800hp at 2,500rpm

Armament: 105mm (4.16 in) L7 tank gun, 7.62mm (0.3 in) co-axial machine gun, 12.7mm (0.5 in) A/A machine gun
Armour: 20mm (0.78 in) minimum, 80mm (3.15 in) maximum

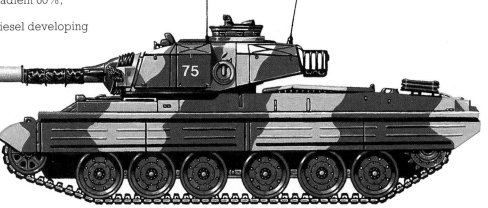

The side view shows the early Mk3, while the photograph depicts the more recent Mk 3 I version.

VICKERS VALIANT

Developed privately by Vickers Defence Systems Limited for the export market, the Valiant first appeared at the British Army Equipment Exhibition in 1980. The tank itself is basic in design although scope exists for the addition of a number of extras. The welded aluminium hull and turret may be supplemented with a layer of Chobham armour although inevitably this will lead to an increase in weight and corresponding drop in performance. Valiant is fitted with a Cendor commander day/night sight, a Barr and Stroud laser rangefinder, a Marconi SFC 600 fire-control system and is offered with a passive night-fighting and driving equipment. An armoured recovery vehicle and bridgelayer are produced as variants.

Type: main battle tank
Nationality: United Kingdom
Crew: four
Weight: empty 41,000kg (90,200 lb); loaded 43,600kg (95,920 lb)
Dimensions: length (gun forward) 9.53m (31 ft 3 in), (hull) 7.51m (24 ft 7 in); width 3.3m (10 ft 9 in); height 2.64m (8 ft 7 in)
Ground Pressure: 0.81kg/sq cm (11.58 psi)
Performance: speed 56km/h (34.80 mph); range 480km (298 miles); vertical obstacle 0.91m (3 ft); trench 2.44m (8 ft); gradient 60%; wading 1.14m (3 ft 9 in)
Engine: General Motors 12V-71T 12-cylinder diesel, developing 915hp at 2,500rpm, or Leyland L60 Mk 48 developing 650hp at 2,670rpm

Armament: 105mm (4.16 in) L7 tank gun, 7.62mm (0.3 in) co-axial machine gun, 7.62mm (0.3 in) or 12.7mm (0.5 in) A/A machine gun
Armour: 20mm (0.78 in) minimum, 80mm (3.15 in) maximum

Top right:
The one and only Valiant prototype takes an incline at speed.

AMX-13

The AMX-13 entered French service in 1953 since which time over 4,000 models have been produced for domestic use and export. Although early variants were fitted with 75mm (3.0 in) or 105mm (4.16 in) guns, all current models are armed with a 90mm (3.56 in) gun capable of penetrating the armour of any light tank but not of a modern MBT. Many vehicles have been retro-fitted with night-vision equipment and NBC proofing, while those in French service are often armed with four SS-11 anti-tank missiles, two on each side of the turret. Twenty-three variants of the AMX-13 are presently in service with the armed forces of over 20 countries.

Type: light tank
Nationality: French
Crew: three
Weight: empty 13,000kg (28,600 lb); loaded 15,000kg (33,000 lb)
Dimensions: length (gun forward) 6.36m (20 ft 11 in), (hull) 4.88m (16 ft); width 2.5m (8 ft 2 in); height 2.3m (7 ft 6 in)
Ground Pressure: 0.76kg/sq cm (10.8 psi)
Performance: road speed 60km/h (37.3 mph); range 350–400km (217–249 miles); vertical obstacle 0.65m (2 ft 2 in); trench 1.6m (5 ft 3 in); gradient 60%; wading 0.61m (2 ft) without preparation

Engine: SOFAM Model 8 Gxb 8-cylinder water-cooled petrol developing 250hp at 3,200rpm
Armament: 90mm (3.56 in) gun with 7.5mm (0.3 in) or 7.62mm (0.3 in) co-axial machine gun and 7.5mm (0.3 in) or 7.62mm (0.3 in) A/A gun (optional)
Armour: 10mm (0.4 in) to 40mm (1.6 in)

Top right:
An AMX-13 disembarking from a C-160 to demonstrate its air-portability.

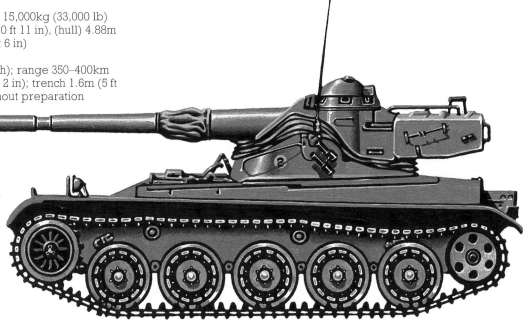

M3 STUART

A direct descendant of the M2, the M3 Stuart entered service in July 1940, saw service with the British Army in North Africa and later with the United States Army and Marines in the Far East. Despite its age it remains operational with several South American countries. The riveted hull and turret of the early Stuarts was later changed to incorporate a welded turret, and ultimately an all-welded hull and turret. Armament consists of a 37mm (1.47 in) M6 main gun, a 7.62mm (0.3 in) Browning M1919A5 co-axial machine gun with similar machine guns mounted in the bow and turret. An M5 variant, with an updated auxiliary power plant and redesigned hull interior, was introduced in February 1942 and the M8 75mm (3.0 in) Howitzer Motor Carriage, with a range of 8,786m (28,825 ft) soon thereafter.

Type: light tank
Nationality: United States
Crew: four
Weight: 12,927kg (28,439 lb)
Dimensions: length 4.54m (14 ft 10 in); width 2.24m (7 ft 4 in); height 2.3m (7 ft 6 in)
Ground Pressure: 0.74kg/sq cm (10.58 psi)
Performance: speed 56km/h (34.8 mph); range 120km (75 miles); vertical obstacle 0.61m (2 ft); trench 1.828m (6 ft); gradient 60%; wading 0.91m (3 ft)
Engine: Continental W670-9A 7-cylinder petrol, developing 250hp at 2,400rpm
Armament: 37mm (1.47 in) 3 × 7.62mm (0.3 in) machine guns (co-axial, bow and turret)
Armour: 9.5mm (0.37 in) minimum, 44.5mm (1.75 in) maximum

The side view shows an early M3A2 used by the US Marine Corps in the Solomon Islands campaign, while the photograph is of a Mexican M5A1 (previously M3E2) Stuart.

M4A1 SHERMAN

Perhaps the most famous tank of World War II, the Sherman, in its many modifications, continues in service with a number of South American and Middle Eastern countries to this day. It has seen action with the British VIII Army in the Western Desert, with the United States Army in Korea, with the Indians against Pakistan, and with the Israelis against the Arabs in 1956, 1966 and 1973. The M1A1 76mm (3.0 in) tank gun fitted to the M4A1 accepts the M42A1 high explosive round, the M8 smoke round and the M62 armour piercing capped round capable of penetrating 101mm (3.97 in) of armour at 914m (3,000 ft.) A number of variants of the basic Sherman exist including the Canadian 25-Pounder Sexton, the Israeli L33 Gun/Howitzer and the United States M10 and M36 Self-Propelled Anti-Tank Guns.

Type: medium tank
Nationality: United States
Crew: five
Weight: 32,044kg (70,497 lb)
Dimensions: length 7.39m (24 ft 2 in); width 2.72m (8 ft 10 in); height 3.43m (11 ft 2 in)
Ground Pressure: 1.02kg/sq cm (14.59 psi)
Performance: speed 39km/h (24 mph); range 160km (100 miles); vertical obstacle 0.6m (2 ft); trench 2.26m (7 ft 5 in); gradient 60%; wading 0.91m (3 ft)

Engine: Continental R-975-C4 developing 400hp at 2,400rpm

Armament: 76mm (3.0 in) main gun, two 7.62mm (0.3 in) machine guns (co-axial and bow), 12.7mm (0.5 in) A/A machine gun
Armour: 12mm (0.48 in) minimum, 75mm (2.97 in) maximum

The side view shows the Sherman Vc with its 17-pounder British gun, while the photograph depicts a typical US M4.

M24 CHAFFEE

One of the most effective light tanks ever built, the M24 Chaffee first saw service during the later stages of World War II and subsequently proved itself a match for the Chinese T34/85s during the Korean War. Despite its age it remains in front-line service today, albeit in modernized form, with several of the world's smaller armies. Although the M24 has no amphibious capability, no NBC system and no infra-red equipment, many importers have fitted their vehicles with both infra-red driving lights and searchlight. A number of variants exist, notably that produced for the Norwegian Army in which the old 75mm (3.0 in) gun has been replaced by the French 90mm (3.56 in) low-pressure D/925 gun, and the two petrol engines by a single Detroit Diesel Model 6V-53 5063-5299 developing 250hp at 2,800rpm.

Type: light tank
Nationality: United States
Crew: four or five
Weight: empty 16,440kg (36,243 lb); loaded 18,370kg (40,500 lb)
Dimensions: length (gun forward) 5.49m (17 ft 11 in), (hull) 5.028m (16 ft 5 in); width 2.95m (9 ft 8 in); height 2.77m (9 ft 1 in) including machine gun
Ground Pressure: 0.78kg/sq cm (11.15 psi)
Performance: speed 55km/h (34 mph); range 281km (174 miles); vertical obstacle 0.91m (3 ft); trench 2.44m (8 ft); gradient 60%; wading 1.02m (3 ft 4 in) without preparation, 1.98m (6 ft 6 in) with preparation
Engine: Two × Cadillac Model 44T24 V-8, water-cooled petrol engines developing 220hp at 3,400rpm (each engine develops 110hp)
Armament: 75mm M6 gun, 12.7mm (0.5 in) M2 A/A machine gun, two × 7.62mm (0.3 in) machine guns (co-axial and bow)
Armour: 10mm (0.39 in) minimum, 38mm (1.5 in) maximum

Depicted in the photograph is a team of Swiss troops practising disabling tactics on an M24 Chaffee.

M41 WALKER BULLDOG

For many years the standard reconnaissance vehicle of United States armoured regiments, the M41 has now been withdrawn from United States service but remains on the strength of over 20 friendly countries. The M41 was one of three main tanks developed for the U.S. Army in the early 1950s and became the prototype for a whole family of vehicles sharing many common components. These included the M42 self-propelled anti-aircraft gun, the M44 and M52 self-propelled howitzers and the M75 armoured personnel carrier. Subsequently a few models were fitted with remote-control equipment and used by the United States Navy as mobile targets for new air-to-ground missiles. Infra-red driving lights are fitted, as is an infra-red searchlight for engaging targets at night. As with most American AFVs of the period, the M41 Walker Bulldog is provided with a hull escape hatch to enable the crew to bail out without exposing themselves to enemy gunfire while escaping through the upper cupola.

Type: light tank
Nationality: United States
Crew: four
Weight: 23,495kg (51,800 lb)
Dimensions: length (gun forward) 8.21m (26 ft 11 in), (hull) 5.81m (19 ft 1 in); width 3.2m (10 ft 5 in); height 3.08m (10 ft 1 in) with machine gun, 2.73m (8 ft 11 in) without machine gun

Ground Pressure: 0.72kg/sq cm (10.3 psi)
Performance: speed 72km/h (44.72 mph); range 161km (100 miles); vertical obstacle 0.71m (2 ft 4 in); trench 1.83m (6 ft); gradient 60%; wading 1.02m (3 ft 4 in) without preparation, 2.44m (8 ft) with snorkel
Engine: Continental or Lycoming AOS-895-3 6-cylinder petrol engine developing 500hp at 2,800rpm
Armament: 76mm (3 in) M32 gun, 7.62mm (0.3 in) co-axial machine gun, 12.7mm (0.5 in) A/A machine gun
Armour: 9.25mm (0.36 in) minimum, 38mm (1.49 in) maximum

M551 SHERIDAN

Designed primarily as an armoured reconnaissance airborne assault vehicle, the M551 Sheridan Light Tank entered service in 1966. By the time production had been completed in 1970 over 1,700 vehicles had been built. The most interesting feature of the Sheridan is its armament system. The short, stubby 152mm (6.02 in) M81 gun/launcher will accept either the Shillelagh anti-tank missile with a range of 3,000m (9,843 ft) or conventional rounds including HEAT-T-MP, white phosphorus, TP-T and canister, all with a combustible cartridge case. Once the missile leaves the gun launcher four rear fins unfold and are adjusted to guide the missile onto the target via a two-way, infra-red, command-link. Unfortunately the gun recoil mechanism has proved too violent for the extremely light aluminium hull, with the result that a theoretically excellent vehicle has proved in practice to be virtually unoperational.

Type: light tank reconnaissance
Nationality: United States
Crew: four
Weight: empty 13,589kg (29,958 lb); loaded: 15.830kg (34,898 lb)
Dimensions: length 6.3m (20 ft 8 in); width 2.82m (9 ft 3 in); height 2.95m (9 ft 8 in)
Ground Pressure: 0.49kg/sq cm (6.96 psi)
Performance: road speed 70km/h (45 mph); water speed 5.8km/h (3.6 mph); range 600km (373 miles); vertical obstacle 0.84m (2 ft 9 in); trench 2.54m (8 ft 4 in); gradient 60%
Engine: Detroit Diesel 6V53T six-cylinder developing 300hp at 2,800rpm
Armament: 152mm (6.02 in) gun/missile launcher, 7.62mm (0.3 in) co-axial machine gun, 12.7mm (0.5 in) A/A machine gun, twin quadruple smoke dischargers

PANZERJAGER SK-105

Designed as a cheap, mobile and well-armed tank destroyer specifically for the Austrian Army, the SK-105 first entered service in 1971 since when some 600 models have been built. The chassis uses many components of an earlier range of APCs while the gun is that mounted in the French AMX-30 tank. The 105mm gun is fed from two revolver type magazines in the turret bustle, each of which holds six rounds of ammunition. Empty cartridge cases are ejected outside the turret through a small trap door in the turret rear. This allows for a very high rate of fire for the first twelve rounds but, thereafter, one of the crew of three has to leave the protection of the turret to reload the magazines manually.

Type: light tank/tank destroyer
Nationality: Austria
Crew: three
Weight: 17,500kg (38,500 lb)
Dimensions: length (gun forward) 7.76m (25 ft 5 in), (hull) 5.58m (18 ft 3 in); width 2.05m (6 ft 8 in); height 2.53m (8 ft 5 in)
Ground Pressure: 0.68kg/sq cm (9.72 psi)
Performance: speed 65km/h (40 mph); range 520km (323 miles); vertical obstacle 0.8m (2 ft 8 in); trench 2.41m (7 ft 11 in); gradient 75%; wading 1m (3 ft 3 in)

Engine: Steyr Model 7FA turbo-charged 6-cylinder diesel developing 320hp at 2,300rpm
Armament: 105mm (4.16 in) gun, 7.62mm (0.3 in) MG 42 co-axial machine gun, two triple smoke dischargers
Armour: 8mm (0.31 in) minimum, 20mm (0.8 in) maximum

Largely unworried by the kind of terrain to be crossed, this lightly-clad tank destroyer packs a formidable punch.

PT-76

One of the most successful light reconnaissance tanks ever to be developed, the PT-76 entered service with the Soviet Army in 1952. Nearly 40 years later it remains in the ambit of several Warsaw Pact countries and is only now being withdrawn from the Soviet Naval Infantry. It has seen combat in Africa, the Far East and Middle East. Fully amphibious with the assistance of two water-jets, one in each side of the hull, PT-76 is capable of operating in any terrain although its comparatively short range would prove a distinct disadvantage in modern combat. The D-56T 76.2mm (3 in) main gun is a direct development of that mounted in the pre-war T-34/76 tank. Capable of penetrating 325mm (12.8 in) of vertical armour at a range of 1200m (3,937 ft) and with a sustained rate of fire of six rounds per minute, the elderly PT-76 can still prove a match for a modern APC or MICV.

Type: light tank
Nationality: Soviet Union
Crew: three
Weight: 14,000kg (30,865 lb)
Dimensions: length (gun forward) 7.63m (25 ft), (hull) 6.91m (22 ft 8 in); width 3.18m (10 ft 5 in); height 2.195m (7 ft 2 in)
Ground Pressure: 0.48kg/sq cm (6.8 psi)
Performance: road speed 44km/h (27.34 mph); water speed 10km/h (6.2 mph); range 260km (162 miles); vertical obstacle 1.1m (3 ft 8 in); trench 2.8m (9 ft 2 in); gradient 60%; amphibious
Engine: model V-6, 6-cylinder in-line water-cooled diesel engine developing 240hp at 1,800rpm

Armament: 76.2mm (3 in) D-56T or D-56TM gun, 7.62mm (0.3 in) SGMT co-axial machine gun
Armour: 11mm (0.43 in) minimum; 14mm (0.55 in) maximum

Waterborne propulsion and steering of the PT-76 is provided by twin water jets.

AMX-10RC

The AMX-10RC, a development of the tracked AMX-10P, entered service with the French Army in 1977 as a replacement for the EBR. The vehicle's infinitely variable hydro-pneumatic suspension coupled with its high speed and amphibious capability make the AMX-10RC one of the world's most versatile reconnaissance vehicles. The 105mm (4.16 in) gun fires a high velocity, hollow-charge shell capable of penetrating 350mm (13.8 in) of armour. A high performance fire-control system with a ×10 magnification laser rangefinder and automatic fire correction control afford accuracy to a range of 1,650m (6,500 feet.) Low-light TV is fitted for night operations.

Type: reconnaissance vehicle
Nationality: French
Crew: four
Weight: loaded 15,000kg (33,069 lb)
Dimensions: length 6.24m (20 ft 6 in); width 2.84m (9 ft 4 in); height (overall) 2.56m (8 ft 5 in)
Performance: road speed 85km/h (52.8 mph); range 800km (497 miles); vertical obstacle 0.7m (2 ft 4 in); trench 1.6m (5 ft 3 in); gradient 60%; wading fully amphibious
Engine: Hispano-Suiza HS-115, water-cooled 8-cylinder supercharged diesel developing 280hp at 3,000rpm
Armament: 105mm (4.16 in) gun with 7.62mm (0.3 in) co-axial machine gun and two twin smoke dischargers

Like the earlier less powerfully-armed Soviet PT-76, the AMX-10RC is fully amphibious and employs water jets, as opposed to propellers for in-water travel.

ENGESA EE-9 CASCAVEL

Cascavel is a fine example of the excellent range of armoured vehicles presently being produced with an eye to the export market by Engesa SA of Brazil. Many of the automotive components are common to the earlier EE-11 Urutu APC. Variants include the Mark I with a 37mm (1.45 in) gun, the Mark II fitted with the French 90mm (3.56 in) H-90 turret and automatic transmission, the Mark III fitted with an ENGESA ET-90 turret and the Mark IV fitted with the French H-90 turret and a General Motors Diesel 6V-53 engine. The H-90 gun is capable of firing HEAT and HE rounds both to a maximum range of 1,500m (4,921 ft.) Cascavel is not fitted with an NBC system, nor is it amphibious. An air-conditioning system and infra-red driving and fighting equipment are, however, optional.

Type: armoured car
Nationality: Brazilian
Crew: three
Weight: empty 11,800kg (25,960 lb); loaded 12,200kg (26,840 lb)
Dimensions: length (gun forward) 5.99m (19.5 ft), (hull) 5.19m (17 ft); width 2.44m (8 ft); height 2.33m (7 ft 8 in)
Performance: speed 100km/h (62.11 mph); range 980km (608 miles); vertical obstacle 0.6m (1 ft 11 in); trench 1.5m (4 ft 11 in); gradient 60%; wading 1m (3 ft 3 in)
Engine: Mercedes-Benz OM-352A 6-cylinder water-cooled turbo-charged, 4-cycle, direct injection, in-line diesel developing 172hp at 2,800rpm

Armament: 90mm (3.56 in) gun, 7.62mm (0.3 in) co-axial machine gun, 7.62mm (0.3 in) A/A machine gun, two twin smoke dischargers
Armour: 6mm (0.23 in) minimum, 12mm (0.47 in) maximum

Designed very much with the export market in mind, the EE-9 Cascavel is in widespread service around Africa and South America.

FV-101 SCORPION

Scorpion was introduced into the British and Belgian armies in the early 1970s and has since proved one of the most versatile reconnaissance vehicles in the world. It has been exported to numerous countries and saw action in the Falklands, where its extremely low ground pressure enabled it to negotiate the marshy terrain with ease. The 76mm (3 in) L23A1 gun, although capable of getting Scorpion out of trouble in an emergency, cannot deal with the heavy armour of modern main battle tanks, nor is it accurate at its maximum stated range of 5,000m (5,470 yards). Scorpion operates within the British Army as one of a series of CRV(T)s. Scimitar, with an identical chassis but armed with a 30mm (1.2 in) Rarden cannon, is used in forward reconnaissance; Striker, armed with ten Swingfire missiles, in the anti-tank role; Spartan as an armoured personnel carrier for specialist groups; Samaritan as an armoured ambulance; and Sampson as an armoured recovery vehicle.

Type: combat reconnaissance vehicle (tracked)
Nationality: United Kingdom
Crew: three
Weight: 7,938kg (17,500 lb)
Dimensions: length 4.39m (14 ft 5 in); width 2.18m (7 ft 2 in); height 2.10m (6 ft 10 in)
Ground Pressure: 0.35kg/sq cm (5.15 psi)
Performance: road speed 87km/h (54 mph); water speed 6.44km/h (4 mph); range 644km (400 miles); vertical obstacle 0.51m (1 ft 8 in); trench 2.08m (6 ft 10 in); gradient 70%; amphibious
Engine: Jaguar OHC 4.2 litres 6-cylinder in-line petrol engine developing 195hp at 4,750rpm
Armament: 76mm (3 in) L23A1 gun, 7.62mm (0.3 in) L43A1 machine gun, 2 × quad smoke dischargers

The side view depicts a Scorpion equipped with the standard 76mm L23 gun, while the photograph illustrates the larger 90mm Cockerill gun mount.

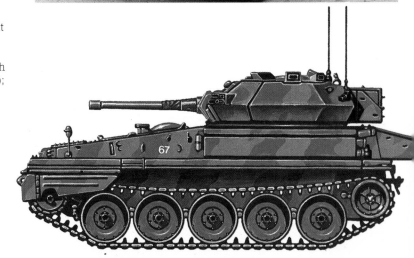

SCHUTZENPANZER MARDER

The Marder entered service with West Germany in 1971 and, despite its age, remains a highly potent fighting vehicle. Designed to accompany tanks under all conditions it has excellent speed and mobility. Firepower is provided by a remotely controlled Rheinmetall Rh 202 cannon with a double-feed belt, a unique rear-mounted remote 7.62mm (0.3 in) machine gun, a 7.62mm (0.3 in) co-axial machine gun and turret-mounted MILAN ATGW missile system. An NBC system, infra-red driving equipment and infra-red/white searchlight are fitted to all vehicles.

Type: mechanized infantry combat vehicle
Nationality: West German
Crew: ten (commander, driver, two gunners, six infantrymen)
Weight: loaded 28,200kg (62,040 lb)
Dimensions: length 6.79m (22 ft 3 in); width 3.24m (10 ft 8 in); height 2.95m (9 ft 8 in)
Ground Pressure: 0.80kg/sq cm (11.44 psi)
Performance: road speed 75km/h (46.58 mph), range 520km (323 miles), vertical obstacle 1m (3 ft 3 in); trench 2.5m (8 ft 2 in); gradient 60%; wading 1.5m (4 ft 11 in), 2.5m (8 ft 2 in) with preparation
Engine: MTU MB 833 Ea-500 6-cylinder diesel developing 600hp at 2,200rpm
Armament: 20mm (0.8 in) Rh 202 cannon, 7.62mm (0.3 in) co-axial gun, 7.62mm (0.3 in) MG 3 rear-mounted machine gun, six smoke dischargers

The Marder seen in the photograph carries a Milan anti-tank missile in its container/launcher clearly visible on the upper right of the turret.

SPAHPANZER LUCHS

Luchs was developed by Rheinstahl between 1975 and 1978 as a replacement for West Germany's ageing fleet of M41s and Hotchkiss SPz 11-2 reconnaissance vehicles. It remains in service in large numbers particularly with the reserve divisions. Fast and fully amphibious, Luchs is unique in having a second driving position in the rear to afford extra manoeuvrability. Although four-wheel steering is normally employed, eight-wheel steering may be engaged in rough conditions. The 20mm (0.8 in) Rh 202 cannon mounted in the turret is similar to that employed by the Marder MICV.

Type: reconnaissance vehicle
Nationality: West German
Crew: four
Weight: 19,500kg (42,989 lb)
Dimensions: length 7.74m (25 ft 5 in); width 2.98m (9 ft 9 in); height 2.84m (9 ft 4 in)
Performance: road speed 90km/h (56 mph); water speed 10km/h (6.2 mph); vertical obstacle 0.6m (2 ft); trench 1.9m (6 ft 6 in); gradient 60%; wading amphibious

Fully amphibious, Luchs employs twin rear-mounted propellers for both drive and steering when in water.

Engine: Daimler-Benz Type OM 403 VA 10-cylinder 4-stroke with fuel injection and turbo-charger developing 300hp with petrol and 390hp with diesel
Armament: 20mm (0.8 in) cannon, 7.62mm (0.3 in) machine gun, two quadruple smoke dischargers